What Every MORMON SHOULD ASK

Marvin Cowan

HARVEST HOUSE PUBLISHERS
Eugene, Oregon 97402

Scripture quotations marked KJV are taken from the King James Version of the Bible.

Cover by Terry Dugan Design, Minneapolis, Minnesota

Notes

1. *Doctrine and Covenants* 1:30
2. *Mormon Doctrine,* p. 764
3. *Apostasy and Restoration,* p. 14
4. *The Great Apostasy,* Introduction
5. Revelation 19:6; Matthew 28:18
6. *Doctrine and Covenants* 1:30
7. The First LDS Article of Faith
8. The King Follett Discourse
9. 1 John 3:20
10. *Mormon Doctrine,* p. 487
11. Ibid., p. 85
12. Ibid., p. 278
13. Ibid., p. 742
14. Ibid., p. 547
15. 1 Timothy 3:16
16. 1 Corinthians 15:1-3
17. *Teachings of Presidents of the Church: Brigham Young,* chap. 2, "The Gospel Defined," p. 15
18. Ibid., p. 18
19. Ibid., p. 19
20. *Doctrine and Covenants* 84:4-5
21. Matthew 7:15-23
22. Exodus 24:7, Numbers 21:14, Joshua 10:13
23. *The Book of Mormon,* II Nephi 29:10
24. *The Teachings of the Prophet Joseph Smith,* p. 194
25. *Doctrine and Covenants* 20:9
26. *Why Mormons Build Temples,* (LDS Pamphlet)
27. *Mormon Doctrine,* p. 780
28. Ibid., p. 118
29. *Doctrine and Covenants* 132:16-17
30. *The Gospel Through The Ages,* by Milton R. Hunter, pp. 126-129
31. *What the Mormons Think of Christ,* LDS pamphlet, p. 2
32. Romans 3:20
33. Romans 5:15, 17-19
34. *Doctrines of Salvation,* vol. I, p. 114
35. *Ensign,* January 1998, p. 18
36. Ibid., p. 19
37. Romans 5:14, 15, 19
38. *Gospel Principles,* p. 9
39. John 8:41, 44
40. Romans 9:30, 10:4, 6, 10
41. *Doctrines of Salvation,* vol. I, p. 134

WHAT EVERY MORMON SHOULD ASK

Copyright © 2000 by Marvin Cowan

Published by Harvest House Publishers

Eugene, Oregon 97402

Library of Congress Cataloging-in-Publication Data

ISBN 0-7369-0231-7

Printed in the United States of America.

00 01 02 03 04 05 06 07 08 09 / LC / 10 9 8 7 6 5 4 3 2 1

What Every Mormon Should Ask

Are You a Christian?

As a Mormon teenager the above question seemed as obvious to me as asking if I were an American citizen when I was born and raised in America. I thought my being a member of the Church of Jesus Christ of Latter-day Saints (LDS) ought to make it clear that I was a Christian! Aren't Mormons known for their wholesome family values, good deeds, and healthy lifestyle? Does any church have a more "Christian" image than the LDS Church? I was certainly trying to be a Christian "by obedience to the laws and ordinances of the gospel," as the third Article of Faith states. I had memorized all 13 Articles of Faith at an early age to help me know how to please God. That's why I was baptized and confirmed as a member of the "only true and living church upon the face of the whole earth."[1] I had been taught that no one except those authorized in the LDS Church had the priesthood or authority to act for God in matters such as baptism, ordination, and temple ordinances.

Although my life was filled with religious activity and good deeds, I still did not know for certain where I would spend eternity. I hoped to make it to the Celestial Kingdom, which is the highest heaven for Mormons, but that required all of the above activity plus "enduring to the end" of this mortal life. A friend asked me how I planned to get to that highest heaven. When I began to talk about keeping God's laws, he quoted Galatians 2:21: "If righteousness come by the law, then Christ is dead in vain." Then he said that Christ did not die in vain because 1 Corinthians 15:3 declares "Christ died for our sins." Instead of trusting Him as my Savior, I was trusting in my religious activity to make me worthy of heaven. Multitudes of other people are also trusting in what they have done instead of what Christ has done. In what are you trusting?

Is the Bible Trustworthy?

The word of our God shall stand forever.
ISAIAH 40:8

The Bible has been the Christian's source of faith and practice for centuries. Believers often call it "the Word of God" because scripture didn't originate "by the will of man, but holy men of God spake as they were moved by the Holy Ghost" (2 Peter 1:21). The God who gave us His Word can surely preserve it since He has "all power...in heaven and in earth" (Matthew 28:18). First Peter 1:23, 25 declares: "The word of God liveth, abideth and endureth forever." Jesus also said, "Heaven and earth shall pass away, but my word shall not pass away" (Matthew 24:35). Therefore Christians are confident that they have a trustworthy Bible.

Yet LDS apostle Bruce McConkie wrote:

By the standard works of the Church is meant the following four volumes of scriptures: The Bible, Book of Mormon, Doctrine and Covenants, and Pearl of Great Price. The Church uses the King James Version of the Bible, but acceptance of the Bible is coupled with a reservation that it is true only insofar as it is translated correctly. (Eighth Article of Faith.) The other three, having been revealed in modern times in English are accepted without qualification.[2]

Mormons usually don't have an answer when asked for examples of mistranslation in the Bible. McConkie's statement shows the Bible is considered inferior to the other LDS scriptures. The King James Version (KJV) is 400 years old, so some of its language is archaic, but it is still a good translation. Although there are several good modern translations of the Bible, the KJV is used in this book because it is more readily accepted by Mormons. But why do the Latter-day Saints use the KJV Bible if it is mistranslated?

For 170 years every LDS president has had the title: "Prophet, Seer, Revelator, and Translator." Why hasn't one of them correctly translated the Bible? Joseph Smith claimed he translated the Book of Mormon by "the gift and power of God" and later translated the Bible by the same power. Both the Reorganized Church of Jesus Christ of Latter Day Saints (RLDS) and the LDS Church have published Smith's Bible, but the LDS Church hasn't made it their official Bible because they claim that Smith didn't finish revising it before he was killed. Why did it need to be revised if his translation was made by "revelation"? It took Smith less than three years to "translate" his Bible and it was 11 years after that when he was killed, so why didn't he complete it? And more importantly, why is the "mistranslated" KJV Bible the only book of LDS scripture that has not been changed? The other three books of LDS scripture have undergone numerous changes between 1830 and 1981, even though McConkie said they "are accepted without qualification." By changing their own scriptures, LDS leaders have shown that there were more problems with them than with the 400-year-old KJV Bible that they claim was mistranslated. While the KJV is an old translation, it has led multitudes to eternal life through faith in Jesus Christ. Have you read the KJV or another good translation of the Bible yet?

Did the Church Cease to Exist?

And the Lord added to the church daily such as should be saved.
Acts 2:47

Catholics claim they are the church that Christ established in the first century. Protestants say because the Catholic Church became corrupt they protested and brought about the Reformation, but they believe Christ's church continued through true believers in Christ whether or not they belonged to the Catholic Church. However, Mormonism claims that both Catholics and Protestants were so corrupt that the true church ceased to exist and needed to be restored to the earth again. One LDS publication says:

> As Latter-day Saints, we testify that shortly after the death of the Lord's original twelve apostles, there came seventeen hundred years of apostasy and darkness. Then in 1820, the resurrected

Savior appeared to Joseph Smith and called him to be a prophet to all the world. Through him came the restoration of the priesthood, the gospel, and the true church: The Church of Jesus Christ of Latter-day Saints.[3]

Or as LDS apostle James Talmage wrote: "The evidence of the decline and final *extinction* of the primitive Church among men is found in Scriptural record and in secular history."[4] That is quite a claim, but is it true?

The word "church" is a translation of a Greek word which means an "assembly." So the church is literally an assembly of believers in Jesus Christ. Sometimes it refers to a local congregation like the church at Corinth in 1 Corinthians 1:2, while other times it is used of all believers of all time (Matthew 16:18). In the Bible, "church" never refers to a denomination or a building like some people use the term today. The church is called "the body of Christ" (1 Corinthians 12:27) and Christ is called "the head of the body, the church" (Colossians 1:18). The apostle Paul used that analogy to show that Christ and His church are inseparable. Just as your head is connected to your body, so Christ (the Head) is part of His Body, the church. Ephesians 5:29 says no man ever hated his own body, but he feeds and cares for it, *just as* Christ does the church. Could the church cease to exist while Christ Himself is taking care of it? Remember He is omnipotent and has all power in heaven and earth.[5] He also declared in Matthew 16:18, "I *will* build my church; and the gates of hell shall not prevail against it." Even after He had ascended into heaven in Acts 1:9, 10, "the Lord added to the church daily such as should be saved" (Acts 2:47).

In John 10, Jesus says He is the Shepherd and His followers are the sheep. The Shepherd goes before the sheep and leads them out, and the sheep follow Him because they know and harken to His voice. The Shepherd cares so much for the sheep that He gives His life for them. That is why He is the *Good Shepherd* and those sheep are the church. Yet, Mormonism claims that the Shepherd lost all of His sheep and had no sheep for around 1,700 years. A Shepherd who lost all of His sheep or a Shepherd who had no sheep for 1,700 years is hardly a "Good Shepherd"! Yet, the Shepherd in John 10:27-28 declared: "My sheep hear my voice, and I know them, and they follow me. And I give unto them eternal life; and they shall never perish, neither shall any man pluck them out of my hand." Are you following the Good Shepherd?

Am I a Member of the True Church?

Jesus said, "Thou art Peter, and upon this rock I will build my church; and the gates of hell shall not prevail against it."
MATTHEW 16:18

I know that The Church of Jesus Christ of Latter-day Saints is the Lord's true church,"[6] Elder Brown testified. But when asked how he knew it was true, he said: "Because it's led by apostles and prophets just like the Lord's original church and because Christ's name is in the official name of the Church, which identifies it as His Church." He also claimed God gave him a burning feeling in his bosom which confirmed that it was the true church. He then urged his listeners to join the true church.

Many people, like Elder Brown, are overly concerned about joining the right church. But neither Jesus nor His apostles ever told anyone to "join the church," nor did they even mention church membership. That doesn't mean that church membership is wrong, but it does mean that some people give it a higher priority than it deserves. A good church can assist the spiritual growth of true believers in Christ, but church membership never made anyone acceptable to God. That is what Jesus Christ came to do, as he said in John 14:6: "No man cometh unto the Father but by me." The New Testament message is not about joining the true church, but about man's personal relationship with God through Christ.

Even though Latter-day Saints believe apostles and prophets are necessary in order to have the true church, the Bible does not teach this. Acts 1:20-22 gives the only biblical qualifications for being one of the 12 apostles. No one can qualify today because he would have had to accompany Jesus from the time He was baptized until He ascended into heaven. Therefore having apostles and prophets does not prove that a church is true. In fact the Bible warns of false apostles (1 Corinthians 11:13; Revelation 2:2) and false prophets (Matthew 7:15; 24:11, 24).

The word "church" is used in texts such as Matthew 16:18, where Jesus said, "I will build my church." He certainly is capable of building it since He has all power in heaven and earth (Matthew 28:18). But His church is more than an organization, it is a body of believers in Christ (Ephesians 1:15-23). The church is called by several names in the Bible, including the church of God, the church of the firstborn and the churches of Christ, but it is never called "the church of Jesus Christ." That name was not used to identify the "true church."

The Bible never mentions "feelings" as a way to recognize truth. In order to know truth, one must know Christ who is the Truth (John 14:6). Do you know Him?

Is God Eternal?

From everlasting to everlasting, thou art God.
PSALM 90:2

George had recently completed his two years as a Mormon missionary when he told his friend Pat that he would make a good Mormon because he was such a good moral person. Pat replied that his moral life was a response to the forgiveness of sins Christ provided for him on the cross and joining the Mormon Church or any other church wouldn't improve that. He said he could worship with any church that truly believed and taught the Bible and his lifestyle would remain the same. George responded, "We Mormon Christians have a lot in common with churches that believe the Bible." Pat agreed that there are some common moral standards but cautioned that there are also some important doctrinal differences, such as what Latter-day Saints believe about God.

"We believe in God the Eternal Father, and in his Son Jesus Christ, and in the Holy Ghost,"[7] George said. "Isn't that what Catholics and Protestants also believe?"

Pat replied that the words were the same, but he believed Mormons understood them differently because another LDS friend who had talked with him recited the well-known Mormon couplet: "As man is, God once was; as God is, man may be." Pat then asked if that couplet accurately conveyed what Mormons believe about God. George conceded that it did and said that the concept came from Joseph Smith, who said: "God Himself was once as we are now, and is an exalted man and sits enthroned in yonder heavens."[8]

"Did God worship another God while He was a man?" Pat inquired.

"Joseph Smith said in the same discourse that 'God the Father, had a Father,' " George replied.

When Pat asked who God's father was, George said he didn't know. Then Pat asked George if he didn't see some contradiction in believing in God the *Eternal* Father, who has a father?

Nothing is more basic to Christianity than who God is, so Christians should question any unbiblical view of God. If Mormons or anyone else are wrong about God, they will be wrong about salvation and other doctrines too, because all doctrine is based on who God is. Jesus declared, "This is life eternal, that they might know thee, the only true God, and Jesus Christ, whom thou hast sent" (John 17:3). If the God of the Bible is the "only true God," then any other god must be false. Psalm 90:2 also proclaims, "From everlasting to everlasting, thou art God." Therefore God didn't have a father. God made that clear in Isaiah 43:10: "Before me there was no God formed, neither shall there be after me." In Isaiah 44:8 God questioned, "Is there a God beside me? Yea, there is no God, I know not any." If God doesn't know about any other god, then none exists, since He "knows all things."[9] Deuteronomy 6:4 says, "Hear, O Israel: the Lord our God is one Lord." Do you know the one true, eternal God of the Bible?

Is Jesus the Literal Son of God?

Whosoever shall confess that Jesus is the Son of God, God dwelleth in him, and he in God.
1 JOHN 4:15

Christians and Mormons believe the above verse, but there is a big difference in what they believe about Christ being the Son of God. LDS apostle Bruce R. McConkie wrote: "Jesus Christ is the literal Son of God...."[10] He explained "literal Son of God" this way: "Christ, destined to be the Only Begotten Son in mortality, was the *first spirit offspring in pre-existence.* He is the Firstborn among all the sons of God—the first begotten in the *spirit,* and the Only Begotten in the *flesh.* He is our elder brother."[11] McConkie also said:

> God the Eternal Father, our Father in Heaven, is an exalted, perfected and glorified Personage having a tangible body of flesh and bones (Doctrine and Covenants 130:22). The designation Father

is to be taken literally; it signifies that the Supreme Being is the literal Parent or Father of the spirits of all men (Hebrews 12:9). All men, Christ included, were born as his children in pre-existence.[12]

He went on to say:

> God the Father is a perfected, glorified, holy Man, an immortal Personage. And Christ was born into the world as the literal Son of this Holy Being; he was born in the same personal, real, and literal sense that any mortal son is born to a mortal father. There is nothing figurative about his paternity; he was begotten, conceived and born in the normal and natural course of events, for he is the Son of God, and that designation means what it says.[13]

To further clarify he said:

> Christ was begotten by an immortal Father in the same way that mortal men are begotten by mortal fathers.[14]

Christians believe that Jesus is the Son of God, but not in the same literal sense that Mormons describe. He is called the "Word" in John 1:1-3, but we don't take that literally. That text states, "In the *beginning* was the Word, and the Word was with God, and *the Word was God.* The same was in the beginning with God. All things were made by him; and without him was not anything made that was made." Verse 14 continues, "And the Word was made flesh, and dwelt among us (and we beheld his glory, the glory as of the only begotten of the Father), full of grace and truth." The "Word" refers to Christ, who existed in the beginning. That is when God was revealed in flesh.[15] Colossians 1:16-17 also declares, "All things were created by him [Christ] and for him: and he is before all things, and by him all things consist." If He was in the beginning and before all things, then He did not have a beginning as a spirit baby in a pre-mortal life. He also made everything and His power holds it together. John 1:4 declares, "In him was life." That is why "He that hath the Son hath life; and he that hath not the Son of God hath not life"(1 John 5:12). Do you have that "life" that only Christ can give?

What Is the Gospel?

Moreover, brethren, I declare unto you the gospel which
I preached unto you, which also ye have received, and
wherein ye stand; by which also ye are saved...that Christ
died for our sins.
1 CORINTHIANS 15:1-3

The Bible proclaims that "all have sinned" (Romans 3:23; 5:12) and "the wages of sin is death" (Romans 6:23). If it were not for the gospel, mankind would have no hope. But there is hope because the apostle Paul declared: "I am not ashamed of the gospel of Christ; for it is the power of God unto salvation to everyone that believeth" (Romans 1:16). "Gospel" literally means "good news." The gospel or good news is that Christ died for our sins.[16] In Galatians 1:7-9 Paul warned that anything else called "the gospel" was deadly. Through faith in Christ's atoning death on the cross, not only are we saved from the punishment our sins deserve, but we also receive as a free gift eternal life with God (Ephesians 2:8-9; Romans 6:23). What a wonderful offer God has made us!

Mormons often talk about proclaiming the gospel, but what gospel is it? In the 1998 study guide for the LDS Priesthood and Relief Society, Brigham Young is quoted:

> Our religion is...the *system of laws* by which the gods and the angels are governed. Are they governed by law? Certainly. There is no being in all the eternities but what is governed by law. The Gospel of the Son of God that has been revealed is a plan or system of laws and ordinances, by strict obedience to which the people who inhabit this earth are assured that they may return again into the presence of the Father and the Son.

Then he said God "has instituted laws and ordinances for the government and benefit of the children of men, to see if they would obey them and prove themselves *worthy* of eternal life by the law of the celestial worlds."[17] Later Brigham added: "The Gospel and the Priesthood are the means he (God) employs to save and exalt his obedient children....Every ordinance, every commandment and requirement is necessary for the salvation of the human family."[18] Later he said, "We receive these truths, and go on from glory to glory, from eternal lives to eternal lives, gaining knowledge of all things, and becoming Gods, even the Sons of God."[19]

Paul declared in Romans 3:20: "By the deeds of the law there shall *no flesh* be justified in his sight: for by the law is the knowledge of sin." And in verse 28 he said, "Therefore we conclude that a man is justified by faith without [or apart from] the deeds of the law." The law cannot justify anyone, but faith in Christ does justify! Galatians 2:21 states, "If righteousness come by the law, then Christ is dead in vain." The law had been available for centuries when Christ died on the cross, so there was no purpose in His death if we could be made righteous by keeping the law. The good news or gospel is not about how well we have kept the law, but about God's free gift of salvation and eternal life offered to all mankind. Have you believed the good news?

Are Prophets Needed Today?

*God, who at sundry times and in diverse manners
spake in time past unto the fathers by the prophets,
hath in these last days spoken unto us by his Son,
whom he hath appointed heir of all things,
by whom also he made the worlds.*
HEBREWS 1:1-2

There is something about knowing the future beforehand that has fascinated mankind almost from the beginning of time. Even pagans had astrologers and soothsayers who tried to predict the future. In Old Testament times, Israel had numerous prophets who gave the people God's Word. But there were also false prophets who deceived the people, so God revealed how to identify them in Deuteronomy 13:1-5 and 18:20-22. The verses say that if the prophecies failed to come to pass or if they encouraged Israel to serve gods other than the one true God, the prophets were false. This method of identifying false prophets is still valid today. But are prophets even needed today like they were before Christ?

Mormons believe their founder, Joseph Smith, was a prophet and that all LDS presidents who succeed him are prophets too. They believe there can only be one prophet on earth at a time, the president of the LDS Church. He becomes the LDS president by serving longer than anyone else in the LDS Quorum of Twelve Apostles. But Old Testament prophets such as Isaiah and Jeremiah became prophets because they prophesied, not because of seniority. Recent LDS prophets haven't prophesied anything. A prophet doesn't always have to prophesy in order to be a prophet, but surely he must prophesy sometime, or why call him a prophet? Joseph Smith and early LDS presidents did prophesy, but many of their prophesies failed to come to pass. Doesn't that makes them false prophets? One example is the "revelation" given to Joseph Smith September 22-23, 1832 commanding Mormons to build the New Jerusalem and temple in Independence, Missouri. It says:

> Verily this is the word of the Lord, that the city New Jerusalem shall be built by the gathering of the saints, beginning at this place, even the place of the temple, which temple shall be reared in *this generation.* For verily this generation shall not all pass away until an house shall be built unto the Lord... [20]

But the generation that was alive in 1832 *did* "all pass away" about a hundred years ago without building that temple or the "New Jerusalem" in Independence, Missouri.

Jesus warned of false prophets who would claim to prophesy, cast out demons, and do miraculous works in the name of the Lord, yet He said He didn't even know them and that they were workers of iniquity.[21] Jesus said in Luke 16:16: "The law and the prophets were until John [the Baptist]." John was the last prophet to minister under the law given to Moses. In Hebrews 1:1-2 the apostle Paul said that God spoke in various ways through prophets in the past, but now He has spoken through His Son. Jesus said, "The word that I have spoken, the same shall judge him [man] in the last day" (John 12:48). Jesus also said, "I am the way, the truth, and the life; no man cometh unto the Father, but by Me" (John 14:6). No prophet can improve that message. Have you come to God through Christ?

Is More Scripture Needed?

*His divine power hath given unto us
all things that pertain unto life and godliness,
through the knowledge of him that hath called
us to glory and virtue.*
2 PETER 1:3

The above verse declares we have "all things that pertain unto life and godliness" and that this gives us an entrance "into the everlasting kingdom of our Lord and Savior Jesus Christ" (2 Peter 1:11). But some claim we need more scripture because our Bible is incomplete. Some claim John 21:25 shows that the Bible is incomplete because it says Jesus did many other things which couldn't even be contained in the whole world if they were all written. Nobody could read that much scripture even if it was available. In fact many people haven't read the Bible through once, so more scripture wouldn't do them any good.

Mormons believe the Bible is incomplete because 20 books are mentioned in it that are not books of the Bible. Books such as "The Book of the Covenant," "The Book of the Wars of the Lord," and the "Book of Jasher"[22] are mentioned in the Bible. However, just because they are mentioned doesn't prove they were intended to be books *of* the Bible. Should the Stoic and Epicurean philosophies be part of the Bible just because they are mentioned in Acts 17:18? To claim that the Bible is insufficient is not consistent with an all powerful, all knowing, and all caring God who gave mankind His message of eternal life. If God cared enough to give His Word to one generation, surely He would care enough to preserve it for later generations!

When an LDS seminary teacher claimed that the Bible didn't contain all of God's Word because of 20 missing books, I asked if the LDS Church had them. This question surprised him, but he had to admit that the LDS Church didn't have them either. He said the *Book of Mormon* claimed that the Bible didn't contain all of God's word, however, and that *more would be written.*[23] Since he used the *Book of Mormon,* I inquired if it was God's word. He testified he *knew* it was. I asked if Joseph Smith was right in saying: "The *Book of Mormon* was the most correct of any book on earth, and the keystone of our religion, and a man would get nearer to God by abiding by its precepts than by any other book?"[24] He said he agreed with that. Then I asked if it contained such LDS doctrines as pre-mortal spirit existence, eternal progression, men becoming gods, eternal marriage, baptism for the dead, and three heavens. Those doctrines are not in the *Book of Mormon,* so it can't contain the "fulness of the gospel."[25] Thus more books of scripture have not helped Mormons explain "the gospel."

While Jesus did many things that aren't written in the Bible, John 20:31 declares, "These are written, that ye might believe that Jesus is the Christ, the Son of God; and that believing ye might have life through his name." Have you found eternal life through believing in Christ?

Do Christians Need Temples?

The most High dwelleth not in temples made with hands; as saith the prophet, Heaven is my throne, and earth is my footstool: what house will ye build me? saith the Lord: or what is the place of my rest? Hath not my hand made all these things?
ACTS 7:48-50

Mormons have built the largest genealogical library in the world because they need the names of dead relatives in order to do their temple work for them. Mormons do temple work for themselves and for the dead. Temple rites *for the living* include endowment priesthood blessings, eternal marriage or solemnizing a temporal marriage, and sealing children to their parents for all eternity. Temple work *for the dead* includes all that is done for the living plus baptisms and priesthood ordinations. Mormons claim that they will do temple work for everyone who has ever lived whether they want it or not, but they won't complete it until the millennium. They believe by doing temple work for the dead they make it possible for the dead to progress to a better heavenly home. That belief assumes that one must join the only true church (LDS) and keep all its laws and ordinances—including temple ordinances—to have God's best in eternity.

Mormons claim that God's people have always been temple builders and they are too.[26] But no temples are mentioned in the Bible from Adam to Moses even though Abraham, Isaac, Jacob, and many other men of God lived during that time. Mormons often claim that their temples are built like Moses' tabernacle and Solomon's temple and are used the same way. But there were no marriages or baptisms in either Moses' tabernacle or Solomon's temple. Mormons call their temples "houses of the Lord" and claim that is where He and His Spirit may dwell.[27] When Solomon dedicated his temple he said, "But who is able to build him an house, seeing the heaven and heaven of heavens cannot contain him? who am I then, that I should build him an house, save only to burn sacrifice before him" (2 Chronicles 2:6). Solomon declared that no building could contain God. He also said that in his temple sacrifices would be burned before God.

Is it really possible for men to build a building that will help provide individual salvation? Can religious ritual such as that in LDS temple rites help redeem us? First Peter 1:18-19 declares, "Ye know that ye were not redeemed with corruptible things, as silver and gold, from your vain conversation received by tradition from your fathers; but with the precious blood of Christ." Are temples built out of corruptible material? Everything on earth is corruptible—temples too! Rites performed in the temple are done by corruptible men and even the rites themselves are corruptible since they have been changed several times. Peter said you *can't* be redeemed with corruptible things, but you *can* be redeemed with the precious blood of Christ. First John 1:7 declares that the blood of Christ cleanses from *all* sin. And Colossians 2:10 says we are complete in Christ. Because of this, no corruptible building or ritual can add anything! The temple of the Lord today is the body of the individual Christian. He wants you to serve and worship Him with your body and spirit (1 Corinthians 6:19-20 and 2 Corinthians 6:16). Are you serving Him today?

Can I Be Married for Eternity?

For in the resurrection they neither marry, nor are given in marriage, but are as the angels of God in heaven.
MATTHEW 22:30

On several occasions I have met with Christian parents whose children had recently joined the Mormon Church and were about to marry a Mormon in one of the Mormon temples. The parents had traveled to the temple believing they would attend the wedding of their son or daughter only to discover that they were not allowed to attend! One Christian parent said, "Mormons claim to be Christians, but no Christian organization excludes Christian parents from attending their own child's wedding! When the LDS Church advertises how important families are and then refuses to allow parents to attend their own child's wedding, they aren't practicing what they teach." The frustration and disappointment those parents experience is understandable. Mormon leaders try to minimize this problem by emphasizing that parents can go to the wedding reception.

But when parents are excluded from their child's wedding and invited to a reception, they feel cheated and insulted.

Mormons try to justify excluding non-Mormon parents from temple weddings by claiming they didn't have a temple recommend and weren't temple worthy. How could the parents become temple worthy? Non-Mormons can never be temple worthy, so they first must join the Mormon Church! Next they need to be personally interviewed by their local bishop concerning specific LDS standards such as being morally clean; being honest; supporting the LDS president as a prophet, seer and revelator; paying a full tithe to the LDS Church; being active in their local ward (church); and keeping the Word of Wisdom (abstain from tea, coffee, tobacco, and alcohol). No question is asked about faith in Jesus Christ, but Latter-day Saints claim that is assumed. Shouldn't they also assume that Mormons already believe and practice the standards required for LDS temple worthiness? Temple marriage is required for individual Mormon salvation or exaltation and it seals the couple together so that they can continue to have children for eternity. It is not only a ceremony for the living but also can be done by proxy for the dead. Baptism into the LDS Church is called the gate into the celestial or highest heaven, while eternal marriage is the gate into the highest level of the celestial heaven where they become gods.[28]

Neither Jesus nor His apostles taught or practiced "temple marriage." The Bible records only one wedding that Jesus attended, and it was in Cana of Galilee where there was no temple. Jesus clearly declared, "in the resurrection they neither marry, nor are given in marriage, but are as the angels of God in heaven" (Matthew 22:30). In other words, they aren't married nor do they get married there, but they are single like the angels. (LDS scripture also says angels are single).[29] The only eternal marriage that Christians will be part of is the one in Revelation 19:7-9 where the church (believers in Christ) becomes the bride of Christ. Will you be a part of that marriage?

Is There Eternal Progression?

Beloved, now are we the Sons of God, and it doth not yet appear what we shall be; but we know that, when he shall appear, we shall be like him; for we shall see him as he is.
1 JOHN 3:2

Eternal Progression" is one of the most important doctrines in Mormonism because so much of Mormon theology is based upon it. It teaches that man is as eternal as God. In his first stage of existence he was an "intelligence." Then he entered the second stage, called the pre-mortal spirit world, when he was born as a baby spirit to God the Father and Mother. There he grew to maturity, chose his earthly parents, and was then born physically on earth—the third stage of eternal progression. At death Mormons go to paradise and non-Mormons go to the spirit prison to await the resurrection. Judgment follows, and then everyone (except a few sons of perdition) goes to the heaven he has merited. The worst people go to the telestial heaven. Good religious people go to the terrestrial heaven. But only Mormons go to the celestial heaven and only those married in an LDS temple go to the highest heaven within the celestial heaven where they can become gods just like their Heavenly Father became a God.[30] None of this LDS doctrine is in the Bible, yet LDS apostle Bruce R. McConkie declared: "Bible doctrine is Mormon doctrine and Mormon doctrine is Bible doctrine. They are one and the same."[31]

Mormons interpret 1 John 3:2 by the LDS doctrine of "eternal progression." They believe the first part of the verse teaches that we are all spirit children of our Heavenly Father and Mother in a pre-mortal spirit world. While on earth in our physical bodies, we don't know everything about the future. But when Christ returns to set up His kingdom in the New Jerusalem (yet to be built by Mormons in Missouri) those who have been married in a Mormon temple will see Him in His Godhood because they will also be gods just like He is.

Believers in Jesus Christ, however, interpret 1 John 3:2 by its context and other biblical texts. It tells us that even though we are now children of God by faith in Christ (Galatians 3:26), we haven't begun to see or experience all that God has for us. It also declares that when Christ returns we will see Him like He is with His resurrected, glorified body because He will then change our corruptible bodies into incorruptible bodies "fashioned like unto his glorious body" (Philippians 3:20-21; 1 Corinthians 15:50-52). While Bible-believing Christians don't believe in the LDS concept of eternal progression, we do believe that God has a great future for us. Jesus said in John 14:3, "if I go and prepare a place for you, I will come again, and receive you unto myself, that where I am, there ye may be also." Revelation 21:1-22:5 describes the new heaven and earth and the new Jerusalem that are promised to believers in Christ when He returns. Will your eternity be there with Christ?

Are All Men Sinners Because of Adam?

Wherefore, as by one man sin entered into the world, and death by sin; and so death passed upon all men, for that all have sinned.

ROMANS 5:12

D o people become sinners when they sin? Or do they sin because they are sinners by nature? Romans 5:12-21 teaches that when Adam and Eve disobeyed God in the Garden of Eden, they sinned. It explains that through one man (Adam) sin entered the world, which resulted in death just as God said in Genesis 2:17. Although the law which defines sin[32] was given through Moses, people sinned and died between Adam's time and Moses' time. Notice the terrible consequences of one man's sin: "through the offense of one many be dead"; "by one man's offense death reigned"; "by the offense of one judgment came upon all men to condemnation," and "by one man's disobedience many were made sinners."[33] Through one man—Adam—sin and death began, and now both are inherited by every mortal.

Mormonism's teaching on this subject is very different. Joseph Fielding Smith, the tenth LDS prophet, wrote: "I never speak of the part Eve took in the fall as a sin. Nor do I accuse Adam of a sin."[34] And LDS apostle Bruce R. McConkie proclaimed, "It is proper and according to the scriptural pattern to speak of the transgression of Adam, but not the sin of Adam."[35] McConkie also says that to believe because Adam fell "all of us are stained with sin when we are born" is "foolish; and erroneous doctrine."[36] Mormons admit that people sin, but not that they are born with a sinful nature. But if man doesn't have a sinful nature, why do Romans 3:23 and 5:12 say "all have sinned"? What makes every person sin if it is not a sinful nature?

If Adam didn't sin, what is the meaning of Romans 5:12: "by one man sin entered into the world"? Could sin enter the world through Adam if he hadn't sinned? The "one that sinned" in Romans 5:16 was Adam! First John 3:4 declares, "Sin is the transgression of the law." Even the dictionary defines "transgression" as "sin." Therefore it's clear that Adam's transgression was sin. This text in Romans calls Adam's action "transgression," "offense," and "disobedience."[37] Verse 19 says, "by one man's disobedience many were made sinners." How did that happen unless we inherited a sinful nature? Through God's grace we thankfully do not need to remain in a sinful condition because Christ came to redeem us.

Who Are the Children of God?

For ye are all one in Christ Jesus.
GALATIANS 3:28

The Fatherhood of God and the brotherhood of all mankind is believed by many religious people. The LDS Church, however, has a very different belief about that concept. At a fireside meeting, an LDS elder explained that we are all children of God. In support of his claims he read these statements from LDS prophets Joseph F. Smith and Brigham Young:

> All men and women are…literally the sons and daughters of Deity…Man as a spirit, was begotten and born of heavenly parents, and reared to maturity in the mansions of the Father, prior to coming upon the earth in a temporal [physical] body.

> Every person who was ever born on earth was our spirit brother or sister in heaven. The first spirit born to our heavenly parents was Jesus Christ. He is thus our elder brother.[38]

But Genesis 2:7 declares: "And the Lord God formed man of the dust of the ground, and breathed into his nostrils the breath of life; and man became a living soul." Zechariah 12:1 agrees with that when it says that the Lord "… formeth the *spirit* of man *within him*." God also stated in Isaiah 45:12, "I have made the earth, and created man upon it." And in 1 Corinthians 15:46 Paul said that man's physical life came first, "and afterward that which is spiritual." The Bible does not teach that we were born as baby spirits of God in a pre-mortal spirit world before our birth on earth.

Some claim Jeremiah had a pre-mortal life because God said in Jeremiah 1:5: "Before I formed thee in the belly I *knew* thee; and before thou camest forth out of the womb I sanctified thee, and I ordained thee a prophet unto the nations." But that verse is about God's foreknowledge. First John 3:20 says God "knoweth all things," and He speaks of things that don't exist as though they did, according to Romans 4:17. God knew all about Jeremiah's future as well as ours. The Bible does not teach the pre-mortal existence of anyone except the Lord Jesus, who is eternal (John 1:1-3). Therefore we are not spirit brothers and sisters of Jesus in a pre-mortal world.

Everyone on earth is physically related through Adam, but that doesn't make them children of God. Paul wrote in Romans 9:8 that just being born in the flesh didn't make anyone a child of God. And Jesus said to the Pharisees, "Ye do the deeds of your Father.…Ye are of your father, the devil."[39] When 1 John 3:10 speaks of the difference between the children of God and the children of the devil, it shows that not everyone is a child of God. Then, how does one become a child of God? John 1:12 says, "As many as received him, to them gave he power to become the sons of God, even to them that believe on his name." Galatians 3:26 also declares, "Ye are all the children of God by faith in Christ Jesus." Have you become a child of God yet?

What Does It Mean to Be Saved?

Brethren, my heart's desire and prayer to God for Israel is, that they might be saved. For I bear them record that they have a zeal of God, but not according to knowledge. For they being ignorant of God's righteousness, and going about to establish their own righteousness, have not submitted themselves unto the righteousness of God. For Christ is the end of the law for righteousness to everyone that believeth.
ROMANS 10:1-4

Paul declared in the above scripture that his prayer and heart's desire was for Israel's salvation. The Israelites were already religious and even zealous for God, trying to establish their own righteousness by keeping the law. But they didn't understand that heaven is a perfect place and only God's perfect righteousness is good enough to be accepted there. Through faith we can have His perfect righteousness credited to us even though we haven't kept the law perfectly ourselves.[40] Since "all our righteousnesses are as filthy rags" before God (Isaiah 64:6), we really don't have anything to offer God. The good news of the gospel is that God "made him [Christ], to be sin for us, who knew no sin; that we might be made the righteousness of God in him" (2 Corinthians 5:21).

Mormonism teaches two kinds of salvation. General salvation comes to all men through the atonement of Christ and refers only to bodily resurrection. No Bible text uses "salvation" to mean resurrection. For example, 2 Corinthians 6:2 says, "Now is the day of salvation." Is now the day of resurrection? All people will be resurrected, but some to the resurrection of life and others to the resurrection of damnation (John 5:29). To call resurrection of damnation salvation is a contradiction. Latter-day Saints also believe in individual salvation, which they often call exaltation. This involves working to enter the celestial heaven where God is, and if good enough, to become a god. This salvation can only be found in the LDS Church and by believing Joseph Smith restored the true church and gospel. LDS prophet Joseph Fielding Smith said man *merits* this kind of salvation "through his own acts through life and by obedience to the laws and ordinances of the gospel."[41] But neither type of LDS salvation is taught in the Bible.

Shortly before Jesus was born in Bethlehem an angel told Joseph that Mary was going to have a son. He said, "Thou shalt call his name Jesus: for he shall save his people from their sins" (Matthew 1:21). The interpretation of the name Jesus is "Savior." Why is Jesus called "Savior" numerous times in the New Testament? Hebrews 7:25 gives the answer: "He is able also to save them to the uttermost that come unto God by him, seeing he ever liveth to make intercession for them." If He saves to the *uttermost,* then we are "complete in him" (Colossians 2:10). Anything added to that completeness would distort it. We are saved "from our sins" because sin is what separates men from God eternally. Romans 6:23 declares "the wages of sin is death" and death is eternal separation from the Lord (2 Thessalonians 1:9) in the lake of fire (Revelation 20:14-15). When we receive Christ by faith we are saved from our sins and the punishment those sins deserve. Then we are given the righteousness of God, which makes us acceptable in heaven. If you receive Christ by faith, you can enjoy all the blessings of salvation too!